A Moose's World

written and illustrated by Caroline Arnold

PICTURE WINDOW BOOKS
a capstone imprint

Special thanks to our advisers for their expertise:
Leah M. Vucetich, Ph.D.
Research Assistant Professor, Wildlife Biology
Michigan Technological University

Terry Flaherty, Ph.D., Professor of English
Minnesota State University, Mankato

Editor: Jill Kalz
Designers: Abbey Fitzgerald and Lori Bye
Art Director: Nathan Gassman
Production Specialist: Jane Klenk
The illustrations in this book were created with cut paper.

Picture Window Books
151 Good Counsel Drive
P.O. Box 669
Mankato, MN 56002-0669
877-845-8392
www.picturewindowbooks.com

Printed in the United States of America in North Mankato,
Minnesota.
092009
005618CGS10

Library of Congress Cataloging-in-Publication Data
Arnold, Caroline.
A moose's world / written and illustrated by Caroline Arnold.
    p. cm. – (Caroline Arnold's animals)
Includes index.
ISBN 978-1-4048-5742-1 (library binding)
1. Moose–Juvenile literature. I. Title.
QL737.U55A754 2010
599.65'7–dc22   2009033360

Moose

Where they live: Alaska, northern United States; Canada, northern Europe, and Asia (In Europe and Asia, moose are called elk.)

Habitat: forests, lakes, rivers, mountains

Food: willow, birch, and other trees; herbs; water plants

Height: 5 to 6.5 feet (1.5 to 2 meters)

Weight: males–1,000 to 1,600 pounds (450 to 720 kilograms)
females–800 to 1,300 pounds (360 to 585 kg)

Animal class: mammal

Scientific name: *Alces alces*

A male moose is called a bull. A female is called a cow, and a baby moose is a calf. Follow a moose calf through its first year and learn about a moose's world.

In the far north woods, the air is crisp and leaves are falling. Moose are looking for mates. A male moose lifts his head and grunts. His huge antlers look like tree branches.

A female moose answers with a low moo. After they mate, the male moose leaves. When spring comes, the female will give birth to a baby moose.

Only male moose have antlers. They can be more than 6 feet (1.8 m) across.

6

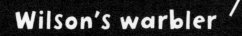
Wilson's warbler

In early May, the baby moose is born. Short hair covers his thin body. His dark eyes blink in the bright sun. His ears twitch as he listens to the songs of nesting birds.

The newborn moose lies still in the tall grass. His mother watches over him and keeps him safe.

At birth, a moose calf weighs 25 to 35 pounds (11.3 to 15.8 kg), about as much as a 3-year-old child.

The baby moose is hungry. He unfolds his long legs and stands up. He wobbles at first but soon gets his balance. He takes a few steps and pokes his head under his mother's belly. He drinks some milk.

Each day the baby moose's legs grow stronger. In a few days, he will be able to follow his mother as she searches for food.

Until a moose calf is about a week old, its mother keeps it hidden and safe in a thicket or on an island.

9

The baby moose is now 1 week old. He stays close to his mother as they walk. When she finds a patch of willow trees, they stop. She bites off some leaves and chews them.

While the mother eats, she watches and listens for danger. She hears a rustle in the forest. Is it a bear? No, it is just the wind. For now the moose are safe.

Bears sometimes attack young moose. If a bear comes too close, the mother moose will kick it with her hooves.

11

Now the baby moose is 1 month old. He begins to nibble tender leaves and grass. He watches his mother wade into a pond. She puts her head underwater.

Moose have big appetites. An adult eats an average of 44 pounds (20 kg) of food a day.

The mother eats plants growing on the bottom of the pond.
In a few weeks, the baby moose will go into the water, too.
He will swim behind his mother.

The baby moose grows fast. By early fall he is nearly 10 times as big as when he was born. A thick, dark coat now covers his body. He hears two male moose fighting nearby.

Clack! They push and shove each other with their huge antlers. The strongest male mates with the young moose's mother, then leaves a few days later.

The mating season is called the rut. It happens in September and October.

Winter has come, and all of the male moose have shed their antlers. Now it is easier for them to move through the forest and look for food. They will grow new antlers in spring.

Antlers are shed from November to January. They drop off, one at a time. The process is painless.

All winter long, the young moose follows his mother. Thick coats keep them warm. They paw through snow to find food underneath. They bite off twigs and bark from trees.

When spring comes, the mother moose gives birth to twins.
Her baby born last year is ready to be on his own. He is
about half grown.

By the end of the summer, he will have his first set of antlers.
They will be small. By the time he is 6 years old, his antlers
will be huge. He will be ready to fight other male moose. Then
they will find out who is the biggest and strongest.

Where do moose live?

In North America, moose live in Canada, Alaska, northern New England, the Rocky Mountains, northern Minnesota, and northern Michigan. Moose are also found in northern Europe and Asia, from Scandinavia to Siberia. The largest moose live in Alaska.

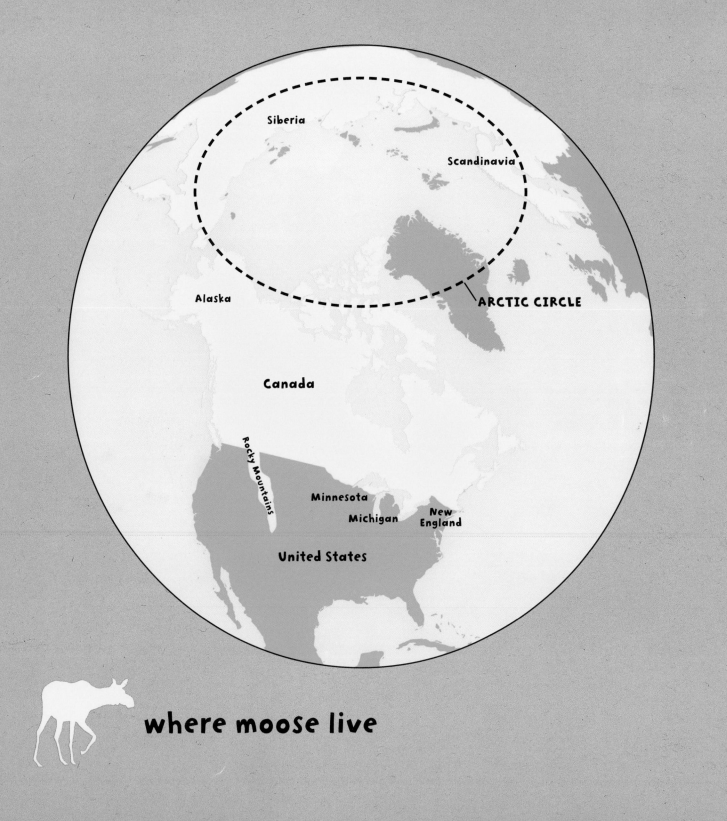

Siberia

Scandinavia

Alaska

ARCTIC CIRCLE

Canada

Rocky Mountains

Minnesota

Michigan

New England

United States

where moose live

Moose Fun Facts

Amazing Antlers

New antlers are grown and shed each year. Each new set is bigger and heavier than the last. The largest known moose antlers are 81 inches (2 m) across and weigh 95 pounds (43 kg). No two sets of moose antlers are alike.

Fast Growing

Antlers first appear in April as small bumps on the head. They are full grown by mid-August. They are the fastest growing bones of any mammal.

Chewing Twice

Like cattle and sheep, moose burp up their food and chew it again as cud. This process helps them digest their food better.

Long Lives

Moose usually live 8 to 12 years, but they may live up to 20 years.

Twig Eaters

The moose got its name from a word in the Native American Algonquin language that means "twig eater." Moose eat twigs and tree bark in winter.

One or Two?

A female moose may give birth to a single calf or twins. She has her first calf when she is 2 or 3 years old.

Big Feet

Large feet are good for walking through snow. Each moose hoof is like a small snowshoe. Hooves are about 7 inches (18 centimeters) long and 5.5 inches (14 cm) wide.

Glossary

antlers—the external bones on the head of any member of the deer family

coat—the hair or fur on some animals' bodies

cud—half-eaten food that an animal burps up and chews again

digest—to break down food so it can be used by the body

mammal—a warm-blooded animal that feeds its young milk

mate—to join together to produce young

rut—the mating season of a moose

shed—to throw off or fall off

To Learn More

More Books to Read

Macken, JoAnn Early. *Moose.* Milwaukee: Weekly Reader Early Learning Library, 2005.

Squire, Ann O. *Moose.* New York: Children's Press, 2007.

Van Laan, Nancy. *Busy, Busy Moose.* Boston: Houghton Mifflin, 2003.

Internet Sites

FactHound offers a safe, fun way to find Internet sites related to this book. All of the sites on FactHound have been researched by our staff.

Here's all you do:

Visit *www.facthound.com*

FactHound will fetch the best sites for you!

Index

photo by Arthur Arnold

Caroline Arnold is the author of more than 100 books for children. Her books have received awards from the American Library Association, P.E.N., the National Science Teachers Association, and the Washington Post/Children's Book Guild.

Caroline's interest in animals and the outdoors began when she was a child growing up in Minnesota. After majoring in art and literature at Grinnell College in Iowa, she received her M.A. in art from the University of Iowa.

Caroline lives in Los Angeles with her husband, Art, a neuroscientist. They enjoy traveling and have observed moose on trips to Alaska and Yellowstone National Park.

Look for all of the books in Caroline Arnold's Animals series:

A Bald Eagle's World   *A Penguin's World*
A Kangaroo's World   *A Platypus' World*
A Killer Whale's World   *A Polar Bear's World*
A Koala's World   *A Walrus' World*
A Moose's World   *A Wombat's World*
A Panda's World   *A Zebra's World*